NATIONAL GEOGRAPHIC

Jeans

From Mines to Malls

PIONEER EDITION

By John Micklos, Jr.

CONTENTS

Jeans
From Mines to Malls

These tough, comfy pants show how American life has changed since the 1800s.

BY JOHN MICKLOS, JR.

Who wears jeans? That depends. In the 1800s, only workers did. Jeans were work clothes. That was all. Now they are everyday clothes. It sounds like a small change. But it shows something much bigger. It tells about changes in our **culture,** or way of life.

LEVI STRAUSS & CO. ARCHIVES (POSTER); JUDPCU SMUKOVSKK/SHUTTERSTOCK.COM (GIRL IN JEANS); © DAVID STOECKLEIN/CORBIS (SPUR); JULIA ZAKHAROVA/SHUTTERSTOCK.COM (JEANS BACKGROUND).

Golden Opportunity. *Miners flocked to California after gold was discovered in 1848. Needing tough pants, they loved jeans.*

A Riveting Idea

Our story starts with Jacob Davis. He lived in Nevada. He was a tailor in the 1870s. He made and repaired people's clothes.

Back then, many people were miners. They searched for gold. As they worked, they stuffed rocks or gold into their pockets. The weight often tore their pants.

Davis came up with a new idea, or **invention.** He put copper rivets on the pockets. Those are metal bolts. The rivets made the pants stronger. Lots of miners bought them.

That Was My Invention!

Soon Davis had a new problem. He feared that someone might steal his idea. He wanted a **patent.** That gives a person the rights to an invention. It keeps others from copying the new idea.

Davis did not have money for a patent. So he wrote Levi Strauss. Strauss had his own business. He sold cloth to tailors like Davis.

Davis asked Strauss to be his partner. Strauss agreed. Their patent arrived in 1873. Then the two men got busy.

Mines to Movies

Davis and Strauss set up a factory. It made **denim** jeans. Denim is a tough, cotton fabric.

Miners loved the sturdy pants. So did other people with tough jobs. Cowboys and carpenters wore jeans. Railroad workers did too.

Movies made jeans even more popular. The first movie studio opened in 1893. Movies caught on across the country.

Films showed actors wearing jeans. Before long, lots of people wanted jeans. They did not want them for work. They wanted them for fun. Even women started to wear jeans.

Fashion Model. *Popular actor James Dean wore jeans in Giant, a 1956 film.*

Jeans Go Global

Then came World War II. The United States joined the fight in 1941. Soldiers traveled all over the world. They took jeans along.

People in other countries saw the pants. They wanted some too. Jeans became popular around the world.

Jeans won even more fans in the 1950s. Rock stars like Elvis Presley wore them. Young fans started buying jeans. They wanted to dress like their favorite stars.

Women's Wear. *During World War II, men went off to fight, so women worked in factories—and in jeans.*

Old Is In. *Clothing companies work hard to create jeans that look like they have been hanging around for ages.*

Big Business

Jeans started out as work clothes. That changed over time. By the 1970s, companies began making "designer jeans:' These had fancy stitching. They had fancy prices too. Yet people loved them.

Today, many companies make jeans. How do they get people to buy their brand? They use **marketing.**

Companies create ads. They try to get you to buy things—like jeans. The ads run in magazines. You can see them on TV. You can hear them on the radio.

It All "Ads" Up!

The ads pay off. Each year, Americans spend billions of dollars on jeans. These people take home new pants. They get a piece of our culture too.

Wordwise

culture: a group's way of life

denim: strong cotton cloth used to make jeans

invention: new idea for making something

patent: government document making it illegal to copy someone's invention

marketing: efforts made to sell something

Ads: Best Sellers?

When was the last time you bought jeans? Did you really need a new pair? Or did you just want the latest style? People buy products for many reasons. Ads target them all. That is why there are so many different kinds of ads.

Copywriters are the people who write ads. They choose their words carefully. With just a few words, they have to get you to buy something. Take a good look at this imaginary ad. Then create one of your own!

Ad Copy

Some kids think playing a new arcade game counts as an adventure.

Not you.

You like being outside, having fun, exploring.

And you need jeans that can keep up.

Headline

Tough. Cool. Casual.
Just like you.

EXPLORER
J E A N S
For the explorer in you.

Brand Name

Product Slogan

Reading an Ad

- Whom does the ad target?
- What is this ad's message?
- Do the words match the picture?
- How does the ad try to get people to buy a product?

Writing an Ad

1. Pick a product to sell.
2. Identify your target audience.
3. Give your product a brand name.
4. Make up a short slogan for your product.
5. Choose a magazine in which the ad would appear.
6. Decide what kind of picture the ad would show.
7. Create a headline to catch readers' attention.
8. Write ad copy that will get readers to buy your product.

Fabrics From Nature

Many clothes are made from natural fabrics. These fabrics come from plants or animals. Find out how they are made. Learn what makes them great.

Cotton

Making Cotton Cotton grows on plants. Workers pick balls of cotton off the plants. The cotton is spun into yarn. Then the yarn is woven into fabric.

Look and Feel Cotton cloth is soft. Some cotton fabrics are thin. Others, like denim, are thick and strong.

Cotton Clothes Casual clothes are often made of cotton. People make cotton T-shirts and jeans.

MAT BARRAND,ISTOCKPHOTO.COM (KNITTING BALL); O'JAY R. BARBEE, SHUTTERSTOCK.COM (COTTON); SUSAN QUINLAND-STRINGER, SHUTTERSTOCK.COM (BOY).

Silk

Making Silk Silk is made by an insect called a silkworm. The worm wraps itself with a long silk thread. Workers unwind the string and weave it into fabric.

Look and Feel Some silk fabrics are thin and cool. Others are very thick. This makes them heavy and warm.

Silk Clothes Fancy clothes are often made of silk. People make silk shirts and suits.

Wool

Making Wool Wool is a sheep's thick layer of curly hair. Farmers cut off the wool. Then they pull and twist it into yam. The yarn can be woven into fabric.

Look and Feel Wool is warm. Some wool fabrics are thin and smooth. Others are thick and rough to the touch.

Wool Clothes Winter clothes are often made of wool. People make wool sweaters and coats.

New and

Dry on the Inside.
Waterproof fabrics keep people dry in wet weather.

Cotton, silk, and wool are natural fabrics. They make great clothes. But they have some problems too. For example, they do not block wind.

So people have made new kinds of fabrics. Nylon is one of them. Nylon is made from plastic. It blocks wind. It is thin too. So it does not weigh very much. Nylon is also strong and does not rip easily.

Staying Dry

Rain is another problem. Natural fabrics soak up water. They get wet and heavy. So people have invented fabrics that keep you dry.

Waterproof fabrics make good raincoats and jackets. They are often made of rubber or plastic. They block water. The outside may get wet. But you stay dry inside.

 PAIGE FALK, SHUTTERSTOCK.COM (RAIN); GORDON WILTSIE/NATIONAL GEOGRAPHIC STOCK (MOUNTAIN).

Improved

Warm in the Cold.
New fabrics let people explore the coldest places on Earth.

Holding Together

People have not only made better fabrics. They have also found new ways to keep clothes on.

That is true for Velcro. It is a plastic fastener. One side of Velcro is covered with tiny hooks. The other side has tiny loops. The hooks connect to the loops. Velcro makes it easy to put on clothes and shoes.

Improving Fabrics

Each day, people find new ways to make clothes. New fabrics do not just keep out wind and rain. They change how we live.

Today, new fabrics let us explore exciting places. People can hike to the coldest points on Earth. New fabrics even let people travel into space.

Jeans

Try these questions on for size to see what you have learned about jeans.

1 Who was Jacob Davis?

2 Why did miners like jeans?

3 How did movies make jeans more popular?

4 How do ads help companies sell jeans?

5 What new fabrics have people made? Why?

BRIAN GORDON GREEN, NATIONAL GEOGRAPHIC STOCK